UNDERSTANDING KUNDALINI YOGA:
A BEGINNERS GUIDE TO TRANSFORMING YOUR LIFE

Santokh Singh Khalsa, D.C.

Based on the teachings of Yogi Bhajan

This book has received the KRI Seal of Approval. This Seal is given only to products that have been reviewed for accuracy and integrity of the sections containing the 3HO lifestyle and Kundalini Yoga as taught by Yogi Bhajan®.

ISBN 13-9781535124362
ISBN 10-1535124369

Table of Contents

Before you begin:

Always consult your physician before beginning this or any other exercise program. Nothing in this book is to be construed as medical advice. The benefits attributed to the practice of Kundalini Yoga come from the centuries-old yogic tradition. Results will vary with individuals.

Introduction

I was introduced to yoga in the early 1970's. It was relaxing and calming and I enjoyed it very much. Looking back on that time, I realize that I did not feel transformed by the experience. It was wonderful while I was practicing the yoga, but I did not feel any different the rest of the time.

In 1974 I attended my first Kundalini yoga class. The class was unlike yoga I had practiced and my experience was very different. As I left the yoga studio, I had a clear insight: the person leaving the class was not the same person who had come to the class. I had gone through a profound, life changing transformation and I had become a different person. But that different person was the real me!

I continued practicing Kundalini yoga several times a week and experiencing a balance in my life that had not been present before. I decided to put this to the test. I stopped all yoga classes for a week to see what would happen. Over the course of that week, I watched as my new consciousness and clarity started to get cloudy and distorted. I actually felt like I was going crazy. I had more anger, fear, and insecurity. I was more reactive to the people around me. This was how I used to feel all of the time! This was when I made a personal commitment to practice Kundalini yoga for the rest of my life.

In 1975 I became a Kundalini yoga teacher and in 1978 I began training other Kundalini yoga teachers. I became a chiropractor in 1979 and began integrating this yoga into my chiropractic practice. My specialty has always been introducing beginners to this powerful yoga. This book is based on my 40 years of experience in explaining the basic concepts of Kundalini yoga in simple, easy to understand language.

This book is designed to give you an overview of the basics of Kundalini yoga. You can study Kundalini yoga for many years and still not know all there is to know, but the basics are simple and easy to understand.

As much as possible, this book avoids the use of Indian yogic terminology. Simple English terms are used instead.

Kundalini yoga is an experience, not an intellectual subject. Having the profound experience of a Kundalini yoga class is what creates change in your life. But a basic understanding of what you are going through can help you to process these feelings and sensations and understand more about how it all fits together. That is the purpose of this book.

The material is presented in the form of answers to questions that a new student might ask. At the end of this book are several appendices with references and links to more detailed information about continuing your practice of Kundalini yoga and meditation.

What is Yoga?

Yoga has become quite popular in our culture in the past 50 years. Even if you have not done it yourself, you are probably aware that it involves putting the body into specific postures to make the body stronger and more flexible, and the mind calmer. How does it do this? How is it different from regular exercise?

In Eastern philosophy, body and mind are seen as being much more interconnected than in the West. Over the last several decades brain research has shown how connected the mental state is to the physical body. Imagine, if you will, a group of scientists studying the effect that different body positions had on the mind and recording and refining these observations for several thousands of years. That is how yoga was developed.

One of the core aspects of Eastern spiritual philosophy is the concept of merging your individual consciousness with a higher universal consciousness. Sometimes this individual consciousness is referred to as the ego or self. There are many names for the universal consciousness: God, Great Spirit, Om, Higher Power, Universal Intelligence, etc. The soul or spirit is the expression of this universal consciousness within every being.

The word *yoga* means union and is related to the word *yoke*, as in a yoke of oxen. The wooden yoke unifies the pulling strength of the oxen. Putting all of this together, yoga is an ancient science developed over thousands of years of how to move the physical body and focus the mind to create a union between the ego and the spirit.

When you are born, you identify with the physical attributes of your life: your body, your sex, your race, your level of intelligence, your personality, your individuality, etc. But within you is a longing to connect and unify yourself with something greater than your individual identity. This is the foundation of spiritual practice. Through yoga you are able to rediscover your true spiritual essence and expand your consciousness so you can embrace both your individual and universal identities at the same time.

Yoga classes are a combination of physical postures, movement, and breathing. Some types of yoga also include meditation and chanting. While conventional exercise can strengthen the body and even promote mental calmness, it is primarily oriented towards the physical. Yoga, while sharing many aspects with physical exercise, is primarily oriented towards the union between ego and spirit. It just so happens that it also creates physical strength, flexibility and mental balance.

How is Kundalini yoga as taught by Yogi Bhajan® different from other yoga?

The most common type of yoga taught is Hatha yoga and consists of postures, some of them quite challenging. This type of yoga is practiced in India mostly by people who have dedicated their lives to perfecting these difficult poses. They have retreated from the world and do yoga all day long and are provided food and shelter by the people around them as a charity. They do not have a job or family or bills to pay. Their whole day is dedicated to their yogic practice.

Kundalini yoga uses many of the simpler postures of Hatha yoga, but the emphasis is not on perfecting a physical pose, but on combining the poses with simple breath techniques, mantras, and meditations to create a shift in the consciousness of the yoga practitioner. The poses are much easier for the average person to perform than many of the difficult poses of Hatha yoga. Kundalini yoga classes have lots of movement and always have a spiritual orientation.

The word Kundalini refers to a reservoir of powerful energy at the base of your spine. Most people barely tap into this power source throughout their entire lives. Kundalini yoga first prepares your nervous system to handle the increased energy, and then brings this energy up the spine to elevate your body, mind and spirit.

The end result is that Kundalini yoga does not need to be practiced many hours a day in order to receive the benefit. By practicing this yoga daily for a relatively short time, you can change your life. You can manage your stress and find health, happiness and spiritual balance. That is why Kundalini yoga is so perfect for a modern 21st century lifestyle.

Why is the Kundalini yoga teacher wearing white and a head covering and do I need to do this?

Physics teaches us that white light is actually made up of all of the colors of the rainbow. Each color is a different frequency. In color therapy, people are balanced by using these different frequencies. The Kundalini yoga teacher wears white because it contains all of the different light frequencies. Wearing white helps the teacher have a stronger projection.

Your teacher is doing more than just teaching the class. As you do the postures, you release old negative patterns from your subconscious mind. Wearing white and a head covering keeps the teacher neutral and protected as they guide the students through this process.

It is optional for yoga students to wear white or a head covering. Some yoga students find that it enhances their experience. Try wearing all white to your next yoga class. Try wearing some sort of head covering. Decide for yourself if this is helpful.

What problems can Kundalini yoga address?

Here is a list of many problems I have personally seen that can respond to a regular Kundalini yoga practice. Kundalini yoga works on so many different conditions because it is not treating these symptoms, but getting to the underlying cause.

Stress
Anxiety
Depression
Compulsive behavior
Addiction
Back pain
Sciatica
Neck pain
Headaches
Migraines
High blood pressure
Digestive problems
High blood sugar
Insomnia
Autoimmune diseases
Allergies
Recurring infections
Circulation problems
Fibromyalgia
Chronic fatigue
PMS
Menstrual problems
Prostate problems
Bladder problems
Low sex drive

What positive results can Kundalini yoga manifest?

Here is a list of many of the positive benefits I have personally seen that come from a regular Kundalini yoga practice:

Increased energy and vitality
Positive and enthusiastic outlook on life
Increased cardiovascular strength
Increased muscle strength
Stronger core
Increased breath capacity
Calmness
Centeredness
Less reactivity to stress
Spiritual awakening
Better communication
Better relationships
Self love and acceptance
Prosperity
Contentment
Neutrality
Joy
Harmony
Peace

Who is Yogi Bhajan?

Yogi Bhajan grew up in the Punjab area of India and was fortunate to work with several yoga masters who taught him the secret science of Kundalini yoga. He came to the United States in 1969 and started teaching this yoga to the public. Unlike most of the other yoga masters who came from India, he was not a monk or a priest. Up to that time, he had worked as a customs agent and had a wife and three children. Also unlike other yoga masters, he was not looking for disciples who would bow and serve him. His purpose was to give people the tools they needed to transform their lives and to train new Kundalini yoga teachers.

Before Yogi Bhajan started teaching Kundalini yoga in 1969, tradition forbid teaching this yoga to the public. Traditionally it had always been taught to just a few advanced students. He learned this yoga as a young man, and was declared a master by his teacher when he was 16 years old. Yogi Bhajan started teaching Kundalini yoga openly because he did not believe in the superstitions and rules that kept these techniques secret. He felt that the time was right for Kundalini yoga to be practiced by all types of people.

He founded 3HO (Healthy Happy Holy Organization) to spread the teachings of Kundalini yoga. This type of yoga is now taught all over the world by thousands of teachers. He passed away in 2004 after giving most of his adult life to teaching and healing people all over the planet.

Why is Kundalini yoga so important now?

We are living in interesting times. This is the end of the Age of Pisces which the world has been going through for the past 2000 years, and entering into the Age of Aquarius for the next 2000 years. What are these ages? Just as a person goes through the 12 astrological signs in 1 year, the planet Earth goes through the 12 astrological signs over 24,000 years. All of the Earth is dominated by each sign for around 2000 years. We have been in the transition to this new age for the last 50 years. November 11, 2011 (11/11/11) was the beginning of the Aquarian Age. Every person on planet Earth has been and will be affected by this shift.

The Piscean Age was dominated by hierarchy and power. Over the past 2000 years, in order for a person to live a fulfilled life, they needed someone or something to believe in. This could be a religion, a political ideology, a charismatic leader, work, etc. The keys to life were hidden and kept secret in the halls of power and in the monasteries and ashrams. But a person didn't need to know these secrets; they only needed to follow leaders and guides who did. Power was held by a very few at the top and it was essential for everyone to find their place in the pecking order.

This has been the foundation for human consciousness for the past 2000 years. Everything that you have learned from your parents, and they from their parents, going back 2000 years, has been colored by this Piscean frame of reference. And over the last 50 years this has completely changed.

The Aquarian Age is dominated by networks, and information. This is the age of information. Nothing is secret anymore. All information is available at your fingertips. Where the Piscean age was organized in a vertical, up and down structure of hierarchies, the Aquarian Age is organized in a horizontal network, opening the world up to true equality. In this new age, the focus is no longer on believing in something outside yourself, but on finding these truths within. It is no longer necessary to be led by others, but to become a leader of one: you. Instead of being a railroad car that is pulled by an engine, you become your own engine. It is your responsibility to stay on the tracks and to keep moving forward.

With this understanding, it is easier to comprehend what has been happening in the world over the last 50 years. On the inner level, since the 1960's, there has been a huge movement towards personal transformation: self awareness, self improvement, yoga, meditation, tai chi, alternative healing, natural foods, etc. There has also been a major increase in depression, suicide, anxiety, stress, and drug use, both pharmaceutical and recreational.

In the outer world, we have seen amazing changes: civil rights, environmental consciousness, women's rights, gay rights, global consciousness, etc. We have also seen the rise of fundamentalism, terrorism, partisan politics, racism, xenophobia (the fear of the *other*), and general fear mongering.

This shift is bringing out the best and the worst in mankind. Some people are preparing for this shift by opening their hearts and minds and embracing this new age, and some people are intimidated by the changes that they don't understand and want to return to a fictional *golden age* in the past, or to circle the wagons and trust only those who are like themselves.

Transformation is never a painless process. When you fast or cleanse to purify your body, at first you feel worse, because toxins get stirred up in order to be eliminated. Once these poisons have been cleared, you feel lighter and more energized. Now imagine that every person on planet Earth is going through this shift.

We are in a time of radical change. It is a time of great potential growth and expansion, and it is also a time of great potential pain and suffering. The more that you understand what is happening, the more that you can go through these changes without losing your balance and stability. Kundalini yoga is a powerful set of tools to help a person go through this transition.

Why is it so hard to change my attitudes and behaviors?

You want to be happy. You want to be healthy. You want to be loved. But when you look at your life, you see that often you do things and make choices that have unhappiness, disease, and alienation built into them. You look within and around yourself, and you see loneliness, depression, obesity, addiction, and self-destructive behaviors. Why do you make these choices? How often have you decided that you were going to make a change, created a plan, and then somehow got lost along the way?

Modern neuroscience has given a clue as to how this happens. You go through life thinking that your conscious mind is in control, but it is not. Everything that you think, everything that you do, everything that you feel, comes from your subconscious. The choices that you make, the words that you say, the actions that you take, all originate in the subconscious. If you have a lot of anger in your subconscious, then no matter how hard you try, it will come out: in a face, in a gesture, in a tone of voice, etc. If you have feelings of low self-esteem in your subconscious, it doesn't matter how positive you want to be about your future, you will act like you don't deserve good things happening to you. The examples of how your subconscious affects you can go on and on. If your subconscious determines your behaviors, how can you make changes to your life?

That is the power of Kundalini yoga and meditation. These postures, breath techniques, meditations and mantras have been used for thousands of years to release the negative aspects of the subconscious that hold a person back. They are a complete set of tools that you can use on a daily basis to reprogram the negative and painful memories and attachments that are buried deep within your subconscious. By releasing these old patterns and replacing them with new ones, you begin the process of healing yourself. As you heal, you are able to make huge changes in your behavior that were impossible before. This is how Kundalini yoga has the potential to create balance, harmony, and success in your life.

What do Kundalini yoga postures do?

Each yogic posture works on shifting your entire being through the movement and position of your physical body. Some postures work because of a certain area that is stretched. Some postures work because the position of the joints stimulates your glands to secrete hormones that balance the body. Yogi Bhajan often said, "Glands are the guardians of your health." Some postures work by strengthening the core muscles. It is helpful to think of each posture as a tool that is designed for a specific purpose. You wouldn't try to drive a nail with a screwdriver, or cut a board with a hammer. Each posture or tool has a very specific purpose. And they all share the characteristic of using your physical body to create changes in your entire being: body, mind and spirit.

Why practice Kundalini yoga sets?

Here is where Kundalini yoga really excels. Every individual posture has a specific effect. A yoga master can combine these postures in a way that the end result can totally balance the body, mind and spirit. This is what Yogi Bhajan did when he taught Kundalini yoga. He designed hundreds of yoga sets and each one was a jewel because it created a complete transformation. Each of these is called a *kriya,* which translates as completed action. A *kriya* is much more than a yoga set. Each *kriya* is a collection of postures that works so well together that their overall benefit is far greater than the results of doing individual postures. A good analogy is the way that a master chef can combine ingredients to make a delicious meal. All of the individual ingredients are tasty on their own, but when combined in the proper proportions by a master, they create something much better. All of the classes that are taught in Kundalini yoga classes were originally taught by Yogi Bhajan. Every class you take or find in a manual was designed by the master as a complete package.

What are the advantages to doing Kundalini yoga in a group?

Kundalini yoga works great when done by yourself at home, but there are definite benefits to doing yoga in a group. For one thing, when you have a teacher leading the class, you don't need to worry about time or what is the next exercise. You can relax into the experience. In a public class you push yourself harder because you see people working hard around you. It pushes you to go further and open yourself up more. But it is important to remember that yoga is not a competitive sport. It is not productive to be comparing and judging yourself based on how you are doing compared to the others around you. Each person in a yoga class is working at their own level and releasing what they need to release. That is why it is recommended that you keep your eyes closed most of the time. Focusing on how well you are doing compared to others takes you away from your own inner exploration and healing.

There are two attitudes that can get in the way of your Kundalini yoga experience. The first is giving up when things get challenging. When you are doing a posture that is getting difficult, it is important that you push through the resistance that comes up from your subconscious. If you quit as soon as it gets hard, you won't make much progress. The second is pushing yourself too hard. If you put pressure on yourself to be perfect for every posture, then you never have any fun, you take yourself way too seriously, and you end up burning out after a few classes. It is essential for you as a student of Kundalini yoga to find a middle ground: know when to push yourself, and when to back off and respect your limitations.

Another reason that it is better to do yoga in a group is that all of the electromagnetic fields or auras merge when you are breathing, chanting, moving and meditating together. This gives you a boost that is easy to feel. There is nothing like the elevation that you feel when doing Kundalini yoga together with a group.

How do I prepare for a Kundalini yoga class?

The most important thing to do to prepare for a yoga class: Just show up!

Don't let this list limit you. None of them are requirements. The important thing is to come and have the experience. With that said, here are a few things you can do to prepare for a Kundalini yoga class.

1. Go to class with an empty stomach. If you are going to an evening class and you need to eat before, eat something light, like fruit or a small salad. You want your blood going to your muscles and your brain instead of to your digestive organs.

2. Dress in loose cotton clothes so your body can move and breathe.

3. In addition to a rubber yoga mat, have something natural to cover the mat like a cotton towel, cotton blanket, wool blanket, wool rug, or sheepskin. Designate this as your yoga mat and use it only for your yoga practice.

4. It is also nice to have a blanket to cover yourself during the deep relaxation. Many times you will sweat during the yoga class, and having something to cover yourself keeps you from getting chilled when you deeply relax. You can also wrap it around you like a shawl when you sit and meditate. It is always easier to stay alert when the room is a little chilly. Wrapping up your body and keeping the spine warm helps the energy to circulate.

5. If your knees and hips are stiff, it is helpful to sit on a pillow and elevate your buttocks. This takes some pressure off the hips and knee joints.

6. Take off your shoes at the door of the studio. There will always be a place to put your shoes. It is also recommended that you remove your socks, but this is optional. Your hands and feet are like antenna that transmit and receive lots of spiritual energy. Practicing yoga with socks on is like trying to get good TV reception with a cover over your antenna.

7. You may want to have tissues available to blow your nose during class. Some of the Kundalini yoga breath techniques can really get the sinuses flowing.

8. Bring a bottle of water that you can drink when you are thirsty during class.

Is what I am feeling in Kundalini yoga class real or is it my imagination?

Doubt is the biggest obstacle that can block you as you begin your Kundalini yoga practice. It is natural when you get started to ask yourself the question, "Do I feel any different?" There is nothing wrong with this question, but it is filled with doubt. You are really asking yourself, "Is this really working?"

When you first come to a Kundalini yoga class, you are like a newborn baby who sees everything that an adult sees, but does not know how to interpret or understand all this new information. A lamp or a chair is just as interesting as a face. But very soon the newborn begins to recognize patterns and make some sense of all of that sensory input. When you start doing Kundalini yoga, energy starts to move and because this is a completely new experience for you, it can be very subtle and easy to miss. Instead of asking, "Do I feel any different?" a more useful question to ask is "How do I feel different?"

In the beginning it is very easy to dismiss what you are feeling as "just my imagination." Imagination is the pathway to awareness. At first what you feel may seem to be your imagination, but as you become more familiar with it, your certainty increases and eventually you gain confidence that the experience is real. At this point, you can test yourself by bringing your doubts back and asking yourself, "Am I really feeling these new sensations?", but now you will have the clarity to move through those doubts. Nothing in Kundalini yoga needs to be taken on faith.

How long do beginners have to practice before they are taught advanced Kundalini yoga techniques?

This is a trick question because unlike many other schools of yoga and meditation, in Kundalini yoga there are no advanced techniques that are held back from beginning students. In fact, one of the most powerful techniques in Kundalini yoga is Sat Kriya and you will find it in the appendices at the back of this book.

In the old yogic tradition, a person found a yoga teacher and he taught them basic yoga. If they served him eventually he would teach them the advanced yogic techniques that he knew. This is still true today in some of the schools of yoga and meditation. Beginners are taught one type of yoga, and only after proving themselves are they taught the good stuff. But when Yogi Bhajan chose to break with the old traditions, he went all the way and held nothing back. He felt that a true master has nothing to hide or hold back, and the only reason to hold anything back was because the teacher had not completely mastered these techniques. Yogi Bhajan loved to play with words and about this topic he once said, "Where there is mystery, there is no mastery. And where there is mastery, there is no mystery." (February 1, 1979)

What is the importance of breath in Kundalini yoga?

When you breathe, you inhale precious oxygen into your body and exhale carbon dioxide. But in yogic philosophy, the breath is also the carrier for the life force or *prana*. Prana or *chi* as it is referred to in Chinese medicine, is the spiritual energy that gives you vitality, and supports you throughout your life. The more powerfully you breathe, the more life force or prana you bring into your body. When you are consciously breathing and holding a specific yogic posture, then this prana is used to transform the mind, body, and spirit in a very specific way. The breath is like the volume control: The more powerful the breath, the more powerful the effects of that posture.

Why am I getting dizzy when I breathe powerfully?

When students are just beginning to practice Kundalini yoga, they may feel dizzy and light headed when they breathe powerfully. This can also happen if they are not using their diaphragm. If they continue to push it, they can even pass out. When I first started doing Kundalini yoga, I pushed it one time and passed out while I was standing up. I fell and hit the floor and had a headache for a week. Needless to say, I got absolutely no spiritual benefit from this!

The nervous system is like the wiring in your home. When too much power is circulating through the electrical wires, the circuit breaker is tripped and the lights go off. This protects the wiring within your walls from burning out. In a similar way, when you start to breathe and the prana starts to circulate, your nerves may not be strong enough to carry this amount of energy so the body makes you feel dizzy and light headed as a warning sign. If you ignore this your own lights can go out and you can eventually pass out. When you start to feel dizzy or light headed, it is important to back off the intensity of the breath until you feel more balanced. Unlike the wiring in your home, your nerves adapt and grow when they are tested. Each time you push yourself by breathing powerfully, it will take longer for these unpleasant sensations to appear. Eventually they will disappear because your nerves are strong enough to carry the full flow of pranic life force.

How does the diaphragm work?

The diaphragm is the muscle that pumps air in and out of the lungs. It draws the breath in as you inhale, and pushes the air out as you exhale. From a yogic point of view, the diaphragm also distributes the prana from the breath to all of the parts of your body.

When you expand your rib cage and relax your diaphragm, the chest expands and air is sucked into your lungs. When you contract the rib cage and tighten your diaphragm, then your chest contracts and air is pushed out of your lungs. This is how you inhale and exhale.

When you watch someone who is relaxed and breathing deeply, you will see their rib cage moves very little, but their belly expands on the inhale and flattens on the exhale. When you use your diaphragm to breathe, it feels like you are breathing into your belly. This is the way your body breathes when you are not thinking about it or when you are sleeping. Yet many people, when they consciously take a deep breath, will do the opposite and suck in their gut and lift their rib cage. This expands the lungs, but it takes a lot of energy, is not as efficient, and causes tension in the neck and shoulders. If you notice that you are lifting your chest when you inhale, then you are probably not using your diaphragm and this creates more tension in your body. If your chest moves only a little, but your belly expands and flattens, then you are using your diaphragm and breathing correctly.

Why do we breathe through the nostrils in Kundalini yoga?

In Kundalini yoga you will breathe primarily through the nostrils, both on the inhale and exhale. There are several reasons why. First of all, you are able to receive more pranic life force from the breath when it passes through your nostrils. In fact, the noisier you breathe, the more prana is exchanged.

For thousands of years, yogis have observed an interesting phenomenon. When you breathe only through the right nostril, this causes you to be more active and alert, and to be more outwardly oriented. When you breathe through the left nostril, this causes you to be more relaxed and introspective. All of these attributes are now known to relate to the left and right hemispheres of the brain. Yogic science is in alignment with modern neuroscience. Breathing through the right nostril stimulated the left hemisphere of the brain, and breathing through the left nostril stimulates the right hemisphere.

You are always breathing primarily through one nostril or the other. Try this yourself right now. Cover up one nostril and see how easy or difficult it is to breathe through the open nostril. Then change sides and compare. Go back and forth a few times and you will usually find that one side is easier to breathe through. And if you check again in a couple of hours, you will find that this has switched to the other side.

This cycle is well documented and switches sides every 2 to 3 hours. Breathing through your nostrils will cause you to go back and forth between a period of being active and outward oriented, and a period of being passive and inward oriented. It balances the brain my giving one hemisphere dominance for awhile, and then switching to the other hemisphere. This cycle keeps you in balance from being too much one way or the other.

What are the main breath techniques used in Kundalini yoga?

There are three primary breath techniques in Kundalini yoga. Here are short descriptions of how to do each one.

Powerful deep breathing: This is used when you are moving and breathing powerfully in postures like spinal flex and spinal twists. As you inhale, relax the abdominal muscles and let the diaphragm descend. To make room for the diaphragm, your abdominal organs will shift causing the belly to expand forward. It will feel like you are breathing into your belly. Let your belly swell out as you inhale. Nobody wants to have a big belly, but this is how to breathe correctly. As you exhale, your diaphragm will push the air out of your lungs and your belly will flatten. The rate of breathing is quick and in pace with the movement of the exercise.

Long deep breathing: The second type of breath is still a deep breath, but is much slower. This is often used when you are holding a specific posture without movement or doing a silent meditation. You slow the pace of your breath as much as possible. You are still using the diaphragm and letting the belly expand on the inhale and flatten on the exhale. Take several seconds to slowly inhale, hold the breath in for several seconds, slowly exhale the breath, and finally hold the breath out for several seconds. Each breath can take from 10 seconds up to one minute when you become really expert at controlling your breath. The slower you breathe, the more powerful the effect will be.

Breath of fire: Unlike the first two deep breathing techniques, breath of fire is shallow and rapid. You quickly pump the muscles at the navel to create a rapid breath at the nostrils at the rate of 2 to 3 breaths per second. To get a feel for the breath of fire, start by sticking your tongue out and panting like a dog. Notice how your belly is moving in and out rapidly as you pant. Once you establish this rhythm, close your mouth and continue the same pumping motion, but breathing through your nostrils. Start at a moderate pace. As you practice the breath of fire, the coordination of your abdominal muscles will improve and you will be able to breathe more rapidly.

Breath of fire is not the same as hyperventilating. If you keep your shoulders and rib cage relaxed and gently pump your navel, you will not hyperventilate. Of course, as was described earlier, any of these breaths in the beginning may cause some light-headedness and then it is important to stop. Once your nerves are stronger, you can any of these breaths for a long time without any dizziness or faintness.

What are Kundalini mantras and why are they important?

Mantra is the science of how sounds and words can affect your consciousness. Just as yogis observed the effects of different postures, they also observed how making different sounds with the mouth and vocal chords affected the consciousness. Mantras affect the mind on a deeper level than spoken language. They have an effect whether or not you know what the words mean. Most mantras in Kundalini yoga are in the Indian language, but Yogi Bhajan taught some in English.

In Kundalini yoga, you will either meditate on the sounds silently or chant the sounds out loud. Here are several important mantras, what they mean, and the effect they have on your consciousness:

Ong Naamo Guru Dayv Naamo
I call on the infinite power of the universe. I call on the teacher within.

This is how you tune in to begin a Kundalini yoga class or personal practice. This mantra is chanted three times. It tunes you to the spiritual guidance that fills this creation, and to the teacher or guru within you. *Gu* means darkness, and *Ru* means light. Guru is that which takes you from the darkness to the light.

Sat Naam
Truth is my name. Truth is my identity.

This is the *bij* or seed mantra and contains the seed or essence of Kundalini yoga. When you inhale, meditate on the sound *Sat* (rhymes with *but*), and when you exhale meditate on the sound *Naam* (rhymes with *mom*.) This simple mantra can be used to unify your entire yoga session into a continuous meditation on Sat Naam. It is also used as a greeting when you meet someone, and as a goodbye at the end of a conversation. You can silently chant this as you breathe the entire day. It is a positive affirmation that helps you remember who you really are. Instead of identifying with all of your temporary and limited characteristics, this helps you identify with Universal Truth. It reminds you that you have this spiritual essence within. You already have all of the answers. You don't have to look outside of yourself for answers. You are already complete.

Healthy am I, Happy am I, Holy am I

This is an English mantra that Yogi Bhajan taught. It is an affirmation that you are in balance on the physical, mental, and spiritual levels.

God and Me, Me and God, are One.

This is another simple English mantra that helps to release negative subconscious emotions. By affirming that you are one with the infinite, it helps you to put into perspective all of the dramas and traumas of our life that can seem so overwhelming. It is the essence of yoga – to unite the ego with the spirit.

There are hundreds of mantras that are taught in Kundalini yoga classes. Another product in the Kundalini Treasures series is <u>Mantras of the Master</u>. This is a CD and booklet with the correct pronunciation and meaning of 64 of the most common mantras.

How does Kundalini meditation affect my mind?

Kundalini yoga meditations release deep hidden wounds in the subconscious mind. As you grow up, you have many different types of experiences. Many of them are positive, but you also go through many painful experiences as well. When you are very young, you are not able to filter out and process these negative and painful experiences. They remain in your subconscious mind buried very deep, like a hidden wound. Some of the negative emotions that are stored there are:

fear	insecurity	betrayal
vulnerability	powerlessness	hopelessness
frustration	anger	rage
blame	overwhelm	despair
distrust	grief	anxiety
hate	doubt	resentment
guilt	depression	abandonment

Even though you may not be consciously aware of these emotions, they affect your behaviors, your beliefs, and the quality of your life.

When your body is filled with chemical toxins, you need to cleanse and release these poisons. In the same way, meditation is a way of detoxing these negative emotions that block your happiness and joy. Many people find that when they start to meditate, their mind starts filling with negative thoughts and emotions. They conclude that they are not disciplined enough and terrible at meditation. The truth is that this means the meditation is working! It is bringing these old negative emotions and thoughts to the surface so they can be released.

When these thoughts come up during meditation, you have three choices. You can suppress them and push them back down into your subconscious. You can engage with the thought and lose your focus completely. Or you can allow the thoughts to come up, observe them neutrally with no positive or negative attachment, and then let them go. When you can allow the thoughts to come up into your consciousness and yet not react to them in any way, they will be released and gone forever.

This is the power of the Kundalini meditations. When you combine a specific posture, arm and hand position, mental focus, breath, and mantra, this brings up these deep negative thoughts so they can be released. And the more that you release these negative patterns, the more that your true identity or Sat Naam can shine through.

What are the yogic energy channels?

Our body has energy channels that allow the prana to flow throughout our bodies. Yoga postures affect this energy flow through these channels. These energy channels are like electrical wires that distribute the life force or prana throughout the body. Each yogic posture stimulates these energy channels in a unique way.

Central channel: When the Kundalini energy rises out of the reservoir at the base of your spine, it rises up through the central channel. This channel is related to your spinal cord. Using postures, mental focus, and specific muscle contractions, you put pressure on the Kundalini to move up to all of the energy centers of the body. When you have blocks in your spine, it is like a kink in a garden hose: the flow of Kundalini energy is severely reduced. That is why it is good to warm up by doing a spinal flexibility series to free up any areas that may block the natural flow of this healing energy. As a chiropractor, I am amazed how close this is to the chiropractic philosophy. That is also why many Kundalini yoga practitioners find chiropractic to be helpful with their yoga practice. As you perform the Kundalini yoga postures, you will begin to feel energy moving up and down your spine.

Left and Right channel: There is an energy pathway on each side of the spine. These two channels correspond to the movement of energy associated with left and right nostril breathing that was covered earlier. Breathing through the right nostril, moves energy through the right channel, and breathing through the left nostril moves energy through the left channel. In some Kundalini yoga sets, you force the breathe through one nostril or the other by blocking off the other nostril with your finger. This actively stimulates these channels as a part of the yoga set. As you get more sensitive to your body, you will feel the energy moving along these channels.

Life nerve: This nerve runs down the backs of your legs from your buttocks to your heels. It is related to the sciatic nerve and the muscles and ligaments in the back of your legs. The flexibility of this area is directly related to the life force flowing through you. That is why in Kundalini yoga this area needs to be stretched every day. It is always tightest when you wake up because it contracts overnight with inactivity while you are sleeping. The life nerve can get so tight in coma patients that their toes become permanently pointed. Every morning in order to increase your life force you need to stretch out your life nerve. Whenever you do yoga that stretches this nerve, it is important to keep your knees as straight as possible and feel the stretch in the back of the legs.

Sex nerve: The sex nerve runs on the inside of your thighs. This is where you store your sexual blocks, fears, and stresses. By stretching this area, you release these tensions and allow your sexual energy to flow easier. This does not mean that you will have an overactive sex drive. In yoga, the sexual energy is related to the ease with which your nerve energy flows. When your sexual energy is blocked, then your nerve energy does not flow as well. By releasing the blocks in the sex nerve, you allow your nerve energy to flow powerfully.

49

What are the chakras or yogic energy centers?

Just as you have many physical organs with different functions, you also have energetic organs that have specific functions. These are your chakras. Each chakra is a spiral of energy that is associated with specific parts of the physical body. Here is a brief description of each of the chakras.

1st chakra is at the base of the spine and is associated with the anus. This is where your reservoir of Kundalini energy is located. Your powerful survival instinct is found in the first chakra.

2nd chakra is associated with your sex organ. Your instinct to reproduce is found in the second chakra. It is also the source of your creativity.

3rd chakra is at the navel or belly button. It is your power center. Physical trainers and martial artists refer to this as area as your core. Power does not have to be dominating, abusive or manipulative. When in balance, it gives you self confidence and discipline and makes you more productive. It is the source of your will power.

The lower triangle: The first three chakras are referred to as the lower triangle. In some schools of yoga and meditation, these are seen as the *bad* chakras because they are connected to the lower aspects of your being: survival, sex, and power. Truthfully, most of the suffering in the world is related to these three chakras being out of balance. But they are a part of who you are and where most of your energy ultimately comes from. To deny these energies is to give them more power. People with no strength in these lower chakras are flighty, and not grounded. To stimulate the energy in these chakras and then move the energy up into your higher chakras is one of the primary goals of Kundalini yoga.

4th chakra is the heart center and is associated with your heart. It is connected with love, kindness, and compassion. This chakra is often blocked from past emotional trauma. If you have ever been betrayed or abandoned (had your heart *broken*), there is a good chance you have put a wall around your heart chakra so you won't be hurt again. This wall blocks you from connecting to other people so it has to come down as a part of your yogic growth. Kundalini yoga works on releasing these blocks.

5th chakra is at the throat and is associated with your thyroid and voice. As speaking comes from this area, it relates to communication. But this is not about day-to-day communication. This is about communicating your essence, or speaking your truth. When this is blocked it can cause problems with the voice, throat and thyroid. Many people have noticed when they start to practice Kundalini yoga, their voice changes. This is because of the opening of this chakra.

6th chakra is at the point between your two eyebrows. This is called the brow point and is associated with your pituitary gland and connected with your intuition. This chakra is sometimes referred to as the third eye because it intuitively sees what is hidden. Most people believe that they have very little intuition, that this is a special gift that psychics or healers have. But you use your intuition all of the time, even if you do not realize it. Take a moment and think about some of the big decisions you have made in your life. Of course you researched and thought about them before you decided, but ultimately you made a decision because it felt *right*. This is how your intuition works. The more you clear the negative voices from your subconscious through Kundalini yoga, the more you will learn to trust your intuition. The brow point is the primary point of focus while doing Kundalini yoga. As you close your eyes, you gently roll your eyes upward as if you were looking at the spot between your eyebrows. This will channel the energy that the yoga releases to open your third eye and increase your intuition.

7th chakra is the crown at the top of your skull where newborn babies have a soft spot. It is associated with your pineal gland and is your connection to your soul. It is the very highest physical point of your body as well as the very highest spiritual point. Imagine at the top of your head there is a lotus flower with 1000 petals. In the center of that flower is a golden throne. Sitting on that throne is your soul. This chakra is the connection to your infinite self. Just as a beautiful and pure lotus flower grows out of muddy and stagnant water, you have a beautiful and pure soul that rises out of your crown, no matter how blocked and out of balance you are.

The Upper triangle: The upper triangle consists of the throat, brow and crown chakras. These three chakras are the highest and purest energy centers and you are always working in Kundalini yoga to bring up energy from your lower chakras to open up the higher chakras.

8th chakra The electromagnetic field of aura that surrounds you is the 8th chakra. Your aura is like a buffer or force field of energy that surrounds you in all directions. It may be only a few inches thick or it may extend out to nine feet. It acts as protection to keep out other people's negativity and judgments. It also acts as an extension of your senses so that you can intuitively perceive the hidden intentions of people around you. If you have a very weak aura, then you are *thin skinned*, you have no buffer, and you react to everything around you. As you expand your aura through Kundalini yoga, you will become more sensitive and yet less reactive to the situations and people that come into your aura.

What are the ten bodies?

We are beings that exist on many levels: physical, mental, and energetic. This is often referred to as body, mind, and spirit. In Kundalini yoga this is broken down even further. You have 1 physical body, 3 mental bodies, and 6 energetic bodies. Here is a short description of these ten bodies.

1 – SOUL: This is your essence that is one with the essence of the entire Creation. It is the spark of infinity within that ties you to the entire creation.

2 – NEGATIVE MIND: There are three aspects of the mind. All thoughts are processed by these three minds. The first is the negative mind. It is skeptical, doubting and defensive. If someone says, *jump*, your initial response is *no*. This protects you from jumping into danger. While it has great survival value, it can be an obstacle to trust and openness.

3 – POSITIVE MIND: The second aspect of the mind is the positive mind, which is the optimist. After having an initial negative response, then your thoughts swing in the other direction, by exploring the question, *Why not*? It allows you to open yourself to imagining all of the possibilities and opportunities. It is the brainstormer within you that can think outside the box.

4 – NEUTRAL MIND: After going through both extremes, the mind can reach a state of balance in the neutral mind. After analyzing defensively all of the pitfalls, and then optimistically expanding on all of the possibilities, the two extremes will come to balance in the neutral mind. Many people get stuck in either the negative or positive mind, but when you are able to get to the neutral mind, you will live in balance.

5 – PHYSICAL BODY: Because so much of your sensory information comes from the physical body, it dominates much of your daily perceptions of reality. Many people don't even relate to themselves as anything beyond this body. It is this body that ties you to the earth through gravity, birth, death, and time. It is also the vehicle which carries the other nine bodies. If you treat it with respect and give it the proper care through exercise, diet, hygiene, etc., it can help you manifest your goals and live a life of happiness, health, and spiritual wholeness.

6 – ARCLINE: The arcline, or halo extends from one earlobe over the crown to the other earlobe. It is the projection of your mind. It is your intuition. It opens your sensitivity to other dimensions beyond the physical.

7 – AURA OR ELECTRO-MAGNETIC FIELD: All living things have an energy field around them that is directly related to their inner vitality and strength. Weakness or holes in your aura will precede illness and disease in your physical body. This field extends out from your body and scans and interfaces with the world around you. Having a *magnetic* personality is directly related to the aura.

8 – PRANIC BODY: Prana is your life force. It is the energy of the breath that activates all of the body systems: circulation, breathing, metabolism, digestion, etc. As you learn to breathe with your whole being, allowing the energy of the breath to penetrate to every corner of the body, your Pranic body is strengthened.

9 – SUBTLE BODY: Your subtle body is the most difficult to connect with because it is so delicate and intangible. The subtle body gives you the ability to know the unknown and see the unseen. It gives you the power to respond to the subtle energy patterns of this incredibly diverse and awe-inspiring world.

10 – RADIANT BODY: This is the highest manifestation of a human being. It is your glow or radiance. It is the part of you that gives you the courage to stand out and be outstanding. It is your warrior spirit, which will fearlessly challenge any obstacle to reach your goals. It is what makes you shine.

What are the locks?

In Kundalini yoga, we contract certain muscles to put pressure on the energy of the lower chakras to rise up the central channel and stimulate the higher chakras. These are the locks. This movement of the energy from the lower chakras to the higher chakras is very important in Kundalini yoga. There are three basic locks.

Root lock

This lock brings the energy up from the first chakra at the base of the spine to the third chakra at the navel. To pull the root lock you lift the muscles around your anus and sex organ and pull inward on your abdominal muscles at your navel. The root lock is always applied on the inhale. After you have taken a deep breath, you contract these muscles. This creates a pressure that lifts the energy from the first two chakras up the central channel to the third chakra. In Kundalini yoga, when you inhale at the end of a posture, you can always pull root lock to increase the power of the posture.

Diaphragm lock

Diaphragm lock builds on the root lock by raising the energy at the navel up to the heart center. Continue to hold the muscles of root lock, and as you exhale, squeeze the breath out of your lungs by pulling the diaphragm upward under the rib cage. This lock can only be pulled while you are exhaling and holding your breath out.

Neck lock

The third lock is at the neck. Unlike the other two locks where you are contracting muscles, this is more about the position of your neck. To create the neck lock, pull your chin inward gently so that you feel a slight tug at the back of the neck. This position allows the energy at the heart chakra to rise to the higher chakras at the throat, brow and crown.

What are the benefits of listening to the gong?

One of the techniques which Yogi Bhajan included in his classes was playing the gong. Usually this is played at the end of the yoga class during the deep relaxation. The sound of the gong is a very powerful technique helping you release deep blocks during the relaxation. It is especially helpful in releasing fear from your subconscious. As the waves of sound wash over you, it will bring this fear up to the surface. For some people, this can be uncomfortable, especially if they are resisting the sound and trying to hold onto their fear. Imagine that you are being washed clean of your fear by the waves of sound, let your fear go and allow the sound of the gong to carry your fear away.

Why do all classes have a deep relaxation?

During a Kundalini yoga class, there are active exercises with short breaks between them. These breaks are to help you catch your breath, but it is also the time when you will have the most powerful elevating experiences. When you are working hard holding the posture and breathing powerfully, there is not much time to feel what is happening. But when you relax between poses, then you can open up your awareness and feel how much energy is moving. It is like the yoga class is a journey. Each posture is a leg of the journey. You work hard to get to the first destination, and then you have time to enjoy and appreciate the scenery. During the short break, you can do an inner inventory and ask yourself, "How do I feel different?" It helps to acknowledge the energy as it shifts.

At the end of the yoga class, there is a deep relaxation. This is the time when you can completely relax and let go. During the class you have worked muscles and joints, stimulated glands, balanced nerves, and released subconscious patterns. During the relaxation, the goal is to get out of the way, and allow all of these changes to integrate into your entire being. Start at the feet and scan slowly up through your entire body, allowing any stress or tension that you feel in your muscles and joints to let go. Once you have relaxed your entire body, allow yourself to go even deeper into a state of complete and total relaxation.

When the relaxation is over, come out of it slowly. Take a few deep breaths. Wiggle your fingers and toes. Rotate your wrists and ankles. Stretch your low back and hips left and right. Finally wrap your arms around your knees and rock forward and back, massaging the spine.

What are the basics of the Kundalini yoga diet?

The choices you make about what to eat have a profound effect on your health and how you feel. The Kundalini yoga diet is a lacto-vegetarian diet. This means that you avoid beef, pork, lamb, poultry, fish, shellfish, and eggs. An easy way to remember this is that you don't eat anything that has a face or a mother. There are many studies that have proven the health benefits of avoiding animal protein. The best study is The China Study. In the 1990s, 6,500 people from all over China were interviewed and examined. Their diet and health status were recorded. These people came from many diverse local areas in China that had significantly different diets. When all of this information was correlated, it was found that the more animal protein in the diet, the higher the risk of cancer, stroke, heart disease, and diabetes.

Dairy products are a part of the Kundalini yoga diet because even though they do produce mucous, this has a protective affect on the nasal passages when doing breath of fire and other powerful breath techniques. For some people, dairy can cause too much mucous and respiratory congestion so they make the choice to avoid dairy products for health reasons.

In the Kundalini yoga diet, people eat lots of ginger, garlic, and onions. These three roots stimulate the lower chakras. Then through Kundalini yoga, this energy is used to open up the higher centers. A recipe for mung beans and rice that incorporates these three roots will be found in the indices at the end of this book.

The Kundalini yoga diet also encourages people to avoid any stimulants and drugs such as sugar, caffeine, alcohol, and other recreational drugs.

A healthy alternative to coffee is yogi tea. This is an Indian spice tea that is very good for the brain and detoxifying the liver. The recipe for yogi tea will be found in the indices at the end of this book.

What is a day in the life of a Kundalini practitioner look like?

Because Kundalini yoga is designed for people who live in the world with jobs and family responsibilities, a day in the life of a Kundalini practitioner is not that different from anyone else. There are a few additions to support the spiritual growth that comes with doing Kundalini yoga.

For the beginner this list may seem overwhelming. Pick one or two from the following list to start implementing into your life. As you are ready, you can add more. These are not requirements. They are simply proven techniques that further enhance your transformation.

Wake up early: The early morning is the best time to do Kundalini yoga and meditation. The day is new, fresh and quiet. There are no distractions that can take you away from your practice. You can start your day in a very positive and elevating way.

Cold shower: One of the most powerful techniques is starting the day with a cold shower. Even though this takes some getting used to, the effect of the cold water on the skin is very healthy. It causes a powerful shift of the body circulation, because your body will shunt your blood from deep inside to the capillaries of the skin to keep you warm. This flushing has a very healing and stimulating effect. After you take a cold shower, you feel completely invigorated and ready to take on the world. The key is to stay under the cold water until it doesn't feel cold anymore. This means that the capillaries in your skin have fully expanded.

Daily Kundalini yoga and meditation practice: Every spiritual tradition in the world has one thing in common: a daily practice in the early morning. Going to a yoga class once or twice a week is always fun and uplifting, but the real spiritual work happens when you start a daily practice. I remember Yogi Bhajan comparing this to taking a shower. You are in the habit of showering or bathing once a day. When we don't do yoga and meditation every day, we start to *spiritually* stink. Start your day by cleaning your mind and your energy field with a daily practice of Kundalini yoga and meditation.

Wearing natural fibers: Because your aura is energetic and electrical, the clothes that you wear have an effect on this energy field around you. It is always preferable to wear clothing made of natural fibers: cotton, wool, linen, and silk. Polyester fibers do not allow air circulation the way natural fibers do, and they create much more static electricity which affects your aura. 100% cotton clothes can be difficult to find, so if you wear a cotton/polyester blend, make sure that the percentage of cotton is as high as possible. It is especially important for women to wear 100% cotton under garments so that air can circulate to their vaginal area.

63

Evening practice: Many practitioners of Kundalini yoga find that a short yoga set and meditation helps them to sleep deeper. This helps you get up early the next day for your morning practice. You can end by meditating to a recorded mantra and let yourself gradually go from deep meditation into sleep. Have the recording play all night long. There are many beautiful CDs with uplifting mantras that you can buy from online retailers in the appendix.

Sleep: You need deep restful sleep in order to rejuvenate your body and also to allow your mind to process and heal itself. When you develop a daily habit of yoga and meditation practice, you will find that your sleep will be deeper, more restful, and often you will need less sleep. I have found that I dream less, and sleep deeper as a result of doing daily yoga and meditation. This makes it easier to get up early in the morning for your daily practice.

Why is a daily spiritual practice so important?

Having a daily practice is probably the most important part of the Kundalini yoga lifestyle. To understand why, you must know a little more about what is happening when you practice Kundalini yoga.

As has been said earlier, Sat Naam is your true identity. You are not a human being having a spiritual experience; you are a spiritual being having a human experience. You are here on planet Earth to grow in a certain way. The challenges in your life are lessons that you must go through so that you can become more balanced and whole. We tend to forget about our infinite spiritual essence, and instead we identify with our body and personality. We develop an ego and separate ourselves from other people instead of feeling our connection. Your ego wants you to forget who you really are, but your spirit is always working from within to wake you up to remember your true spiritual nature. This means there is an ongoing battle within you between the ego and the spirit.

When you go to a Kundalini yoga class, you wake up your spirit and start to remember who you really are, and this is threatening to your ego. Your ego desperately wants to find a way to sabotage your spiritual growth because the more you grow spiritually, the less power your ego has to control you. Have you ever noticed in your past that you started doing something new and it was really great and exciting, and you loved doing it, and then six months later you realized that you had stopped doing it and you had no idea why? This is the power of your ego to sabotage your growth.

When you choose to roll out of that cozy bed to do Kundalini yoga in the morning instead of sleeping in, that is a choice to not let your ego control you. That is a choice to consciously work on yourself every day. That is a choice to create a new habit of growth, elevation, and expansion. That is why a daily spiritual practice is so important. Making that choice on a daily basis is the difference between living a life of separation, pain and stress and living a life of consciousness, empowerment and joy.

How does Kundalini yoga promote self-healing?

Within you is an intelligence that guided your growth from a fertilized egg into a complex creature of trillions of cells. This intelligence is still within you. It is constantly regulating your hormones, repairing your damaged cells, digesting your food, distributing the nutrients to your cells, removing the waste from your cells, excreting this waste, fighting off attacks from foreign viruses and bacteria, and countless other biological processes that go on every moment of your life without a single thought from you. If you are not expressing perfect health, it is not because your body does not know what to do, it is because something is interfering with your innate intelligence.

One of the benefits of Kundalini yoga is removing that interference and allowing your body to heal itself. The physical yoga has a powerful strengthening effect on your muscles and posture. The yoga stimulates your digestion and balances your hormones. The meditation clears out your negative subconscious patterns that promote stress and disease. The more empowered you become to live as the spiritual being that you are, the healthier you become. That is why Yogi Bhajan named the organization that teaches Kundalini yoga throughout the world as 3HO – Healthy Happy Holy Organization.

What is the connection between Kundalini yoga and prosperity?

There is a sad misunderstanding about spirituality in our modern culture: it is more spiritual to be poor. There are certainly many examples of how money can corrupt a person and make them superficial and materialistic. But this does not mean that prosperity is contrary in any way to spiritual values. In fact, prosperity, like health, is available to all people. And just as poor health is a sign of some block that is not allowing your inner healing to happen, poverty and lack is also a sign of blocked energy.

Two negative programs that you may have running in your subconscious is either that you are not good enough to deserve abundance and prosperity, or that money is evil and your spirit will be corrupted by it. Both of these concepts are negative thought patterns that block you from experiencing abundance.

In Kundalini yoga, you learn to live within the world, experiencing all of the gifts of this world, but because you identify with your spirit, you are not attached to these gifts. They do not define you, so they can't corrupt you. Your work in this world is exactly what you came here to do, and you do it the best that you can, and you are rewarded for your work with prosperity and abundance. As you practice Kundalini yoga, you will heal and release the old negative thoughts that promote a poverty consciousness, and then you will find that prosperity and abundance flow effortlessly to you.

What is White Tantric Yoga?

When Yogi Bhajan came to teach Kundalini yoga, he also introduced White Tantric yoga. This was a unique yoga that could only be practiced in his presence. As powerful as Kundalini yoga was, White Tantric yoga was even more powerful at clearing subconscious mental blocks. White Tantric yoga is always done with a partner. You sit facing your partner and go through a day-long experience of meditation and chanting. Yogi Bhajan is present to regulate and balance this healing. You are using the power of the energetic link between you and your partner to go even deeper to clear out your old subconscious negative patterns.

As Yogi Bhajan aged, the stress on his physical body was so extreme that he had to stop leading White Tantric yoga for a short time. It was during this time that he discovered that he could lead these courses without being physically present. He could regulate the White Tantric energy through his subtle body without causing stress to his physical body. He created a library of White Tantric videos that continue to be taught today. He stated that even after he died, his subtle body would still be present to regulate the White Tantric yoga experience.

I have done White Tantric yoga with Yogi Bhajan present physically, and also with him not physically present, but regulating the Tantric energy through his subtle body. Many students ask me if they felt different. I have had many profound healing experiences in Tantric yoga, some when he was present and some when he was not. Even when he was not physically present, I could definitely feel his vibration. Based on my experience, the healing effect has been the same.

What is the connection between Kundalini yoga and the Sikh religion?

Yogi Bhajan was a member of the Sikh religion. When he first came to the United States, some of his yoga students were curious about why he did not cut his hair or shave his beard, and why he wore a turban. He introduced them to the Sikh religion, and some of these students then became Sikhs. But many of his students were happy to continue practicing the yoga without becoming Sikhs. He also explained that many of the mantras that had been used for thousands of years as a part of the yogic tradition were incorporated into the 500-year-old Sikh religion.

Kundalini yoga is not a part of the Sikh religion. There are Kundalini yoga practitioners and teachers of every religion: Catholic, Hindu, Protestant, Jewish, Muslim, Buddhist, and yes, Sikh. Kundalini yoga is a spiritual tradition that is not associated with any religion. People who have a strong connection to their religion find that Kundalini yoga brings new life and vitality to whatever religion they practice.

How can I get started?

If you haven't already found a Kundalini yoga class to attend, that is your first priority. This book gives you a basic understanding of Kundalini yoga. Please refer to the links at the end of this book to find a Kundalini yoga center or teacher near you.

If there are none, there are online yoga classes, videos, and manuals that you can order.

If you are just getting started, go to as many classes as you can in the beginning. Experience as many different teachers, as each teacher has a different style and you may find a better match with certain teachers.

Transforming your life with Kundalini yoga is simple, but it is not easy. As you progress, you WILL meet inner resistance. It can come in many forms:

- You don't like the incense that the teacher burned.
- The music they played was not to your liking.
- The person doing yoga next to you had body odor.
- You got sick and lost your momentum and had trouble getting it back.
- The class was too crowded.
- The class was not crowded enough.
- You read something negative about yoga and it caused you to have doubts.

The resistance will come and if you are not prepared for it, it can derail you. If you know that it is coming and are ready for it, you can sail through it like a hot knife through butter. The resistance is like a paper tiger. It seems very intimidating and fierce until you go through it and see how insubstantial it actually is.

One form of resistance that comes up about doing Kundalini yoga is that you convince yourself that you won't do it correctly on your own. You decide that you are going to wait until you reach a certain level of proficiency before you start doing it at home. Guess what? You probably won't ever reach that level of proficiency if you don't just get started. There is a saying, "Anything worth doing is worth doing well." This may be true in some context, but in this case, it is exactly wrong. A better saying is, "Anything worth doing is worth doing poorly." If it is worth doing yoga on your own, it is worth doing even if you do it incorrectly at first. Because by continuing to practice, you will correct your errors and gradually do it well. But if you are reluctant to start because of a lack of knowledge or insecurity, you may never improve.

Many people want to know how much time they must dedicate to their daily Kundalini yoga practice. The simple answer is anything is better than nothing. If all you can do is a few warm-ups and a short meditation, then get started with that. What is important is to pick an amount of time that you can maintain every day to establish a new habit pattern. It takes 40 days to create a new habit. You will go through lots of challenges in those 40 days, but if you keep up, it will get easier. Eventually it will feel unnatural for you to start your day without your daily practice, just as it would be to start your day without brushing your teeth or showering. For most people, 30 to 60 minutes is a good amount of time. If you are highly motivated, you can dedicate up to 1/10th of your day or 2 ½ hours. And while the best time for the daily practice is the morning, if you can't practice in the morning, find a time that you can, and do it every day.

As a part of this Kundalini Treasures series, there is a CD and booklet called A Simple Yoga Practice. The booklet shows you the postures and the CD guides you just as if you were in a yoga class. This is a way to get started. It is designed to be modular and grow with you as your practice grows. You can start with 15-20 minutes by listening to only the first few tracks. As you want to do more, you can listen to more tracks. With this CD you can increase up to a whole hour of practice.

Long time sun: projecting your healing light

All Kundalini classes end with a simple song that Yogi Bhajan incorporated into the yoga class format from the very beginning. The words to the song are:

May the long time sun shine upon you.
All love surround you.
And the pure light within you,
Guide your way on.
Sat Naam

When you sing this song at the end of a class, you are usually feeling very uplifted and blessed. You have done a powerful Kundalini yoga set, followed by a deep relaxation and a healing meditation. As you sing this song, picture a loved one who needs support and healing. Instead of seeing them as sick, depressed, and in crisis, take some of that blissful energy that you are feeling and project it to them from your heart. See them surrounded by the light of the sun, glowing with health, vitality, and peace. Hold this mental image as you sing this song. You will be sending them this healing light as a gift from your heart.

After you chant the final Sat Naam, bow forward and feel grateful for the opportunity to heal yourself through this yoga. See your yoga teacher sitting before you. See Yogi Bhajan sitting behind this teacher, and see his teacher behind him. See this chain of teachers that have passed this technology forward to you through the ages. Bow to this golden chain of teachers. And bow to your own inner teacher that has guided you to this class. Accept these gifts with humility and grace.

Sat Naam

Basic Spinal Energy Series

1) Spinal Flex. Sit in Easy Pose. Grab the ankles with both hands and deeply inhale. Flex the spine forward and lift the chest up. On the exhale, flex the spine backwards. Keep the head level so it does not "flip-flop." Repeat 108 times. Rest 1 minute. Spinal flex greatly alters the proportions and strengths of alpha, theta and delta waves.

2) Spinal Flex. Sit on the heels. Place the hands flat on the thighs. Flex spine forward with the inhale, backward with the exhale. Mentally vibrate Sat on the inhale, Nam on the exhale. Repeat 108 times. Rest 2 minutes.

3) Spinal Twist. In Easy Pose, grasp the shoulders with fingers in front, thumbs in back. Inhale and twist to the left, exhale and twist to the right. Continue 26 times and inhale facing forward. Rest 1 minute.

4) Bear Grip. Curl the finger of each hand and lock them together at the heart center. Move the elbows in a see-saw motion, inhaling as the left elbow comes up and exhaling as the right elbow comes up. Continue 26 times and inhale, exhale, pull the root lock. Relax 30 seconds.

5) Spinal Flex. In Easy Pose, grasp the knees firmly. Keeping the elbows straight, begin to flex the upper spine. Inhale forward, exhale back. Repeat 108 times. Rest 1 minute.

6) Shoulder Shrugs. Shrug both shoulders up on the inhale, down on the exhale. Do this for 1 to 2 minutes. Inhale and hold 15 seconds with shoulders pressed up. Relax the shoulders.

7) Neck Rolls. Roll the neck slowly to the right 5 times, then to the left 5 times. Inhale, and bring the neck straight.

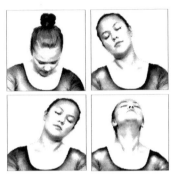

8) Bear Grip. Lock the fingers in Bear Grip at the throat level. Inhale—apply root lock. Exhale—apply root lock. Then raise the hands above the top of the head. Inhale—apply root lock. Exhale—apply root lock. Repeat the cycle 2 more times.

9) Sat Kriya. Sit on the heels with the arms overhead and palms together. Interlace the fingers except for the index fingers, which point straight up. Men cross the right thumb over the left thumb: women cross the left thumb over the right. Chant SAT and pull the Navel Point in: chant NAAM and relax it. Continue powerfully with a steady rhythm for at least 3 minutes, then inhale, apply root lock and squeeze the energy from the base of the spine to the top of the skull. Exhale, hold the breath out and apply all the locks. Inhale and relax.

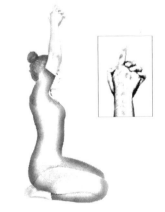

10) Relax completely on your back for 15 minutes

COMMENTS: Age is measured by the flexibility of the spine: to stay young, stay flexible. This series works systematically from the base of the spine to the top. All 26 vertebrae receive stimulation and all the chakras receive a burst of energy. This makes it a good series to do before meditation. Many people report greater mental clarity after regular practice of this kriya. A contributing factor is the increased circulation of the spinal fluid, which is crucially linked to having a good memory. If you are a beginner, you can reduce the times and number of repetitions. The rests between exercises can also be increased.

Kriya for Elevation

This easy set of exercises is excellent as a tune-up. It systematically exercises the spine and aids in the circulation of prana to balance the chakras.

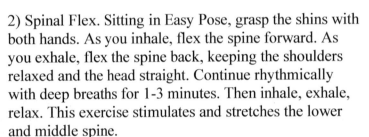

1) Ego Eradicator. Sit in Easy Pose. Raise the arms to a 60 degree angle. Curl the fingertips onto the pads of the palms. Stretch the thumbs so they point upward and inward. Eyes closed, concentrate above the head and do Breath of Fire. 1-3 minutes. To end, inhale and touch the thumbs together above the head, and open the fingers. Exhale and apply root lock. Inhale and relax. This exercise opens the lungs, brings the hemispheres of the brain to a state of alertness, and consolidates the magnetic field.

2) Spinal Flex. Sitting in Easy Pose, grasp the shins with both hands. As you inhale, flex the spine forward. As you exhale, flex the spine back, keeping the shoulders relaxed and the head straight. Continue rhythmically with deep breaths for 1-3 minutes. Then inhale, exhale, relax. This exercise stimulates and stretches the lower and middle spine.

3) Spinal Twist. In Easy Pose, grab the shoulders, with the thumbs in back and the fingers in front. Keep the elbows high. with the arms parallel to the ground. Inhale as you twist to the left. Exhale as you twist to the right. Continue for 1-4 minutes. To end, inhale, facing straight forward. Exhale and relax. This exercise stimulates and stretches the lower and middle spine.

4) Front Life Nerve Stretch. Stretch both legs straight out in front. Keep your knees straight even if you cannot reach your toes. If you can, grab the toes by wrapping your index and middle finger around the big toe and pressing the big toe nail with your thumbs. Inhale the upper body up, keeping the spine straight. Exhale the chest towards the thighs. Bend from the hips and not at the waist. Continue with deep, powerful breathing for 1-3 minutes. Inhale up and hold the breath briefly. Stay up and exhale completely, holding the breath out briefly. Inhale and relax. This exercise works on the lower and upper spine.

5) Modified Maha Mudra. Sit on the right heel with the left leg extended forward. Beginners can put the right foot against the left inner thigh. Keep the left knee straight even if you can't reach your toes. Grasp the big toe of the left foot with both hands. applying a pressure against the toenail. Exhale and bring the elbows to the ground as you lengthen the core of the spine, bending forward from the navel, continuing to lengthen the spine. Lastly, bring head to knee. Hold, with Breath of Fire for 1-2 minutes. Inhale. Exhale and stretch the head and torso forward and down. Hold the breath out briefly. Inhale, switch legs and repeat the exercise. Relax. This exercise helps elimination, stretches the sciatic nerve and brings circulation to the upper torso.

6) Sex Nerve Stretch. Spread the legs wide, keeping the knees straight, grasp the toes as in Exercise 4. If you can reach the toes, keep the hands resting on the legs. Inhale and stretch the spine straight, pulling back on the toes. Exhale and, bending at the waist, bring the head down to the left knee. Inhale up in the center position and exhale down, bringing up the head to the right knee. Continue with powerful breathing for 1-2 minutes. Then inhale up in the center position and exhale, bending straight forward from the waist touching the forehead to the floor. Continue this up and down motion for 1 minute, then inhale up stretching the spine straight. Exhale and bring the forehead to the floor. Hold the breath out briefly as you stretch forward and down. Inhale and relax. This exercise develops flexibility of the lower spine and sacrum and charges the magnetic field.

7) Cobra Pose. Lie on the stomach with the palms flat on the floor under the shoulders. The heels are together with the soles of the feet facing up. Inhale into Cobra Pose, arching the spine vertebra by vertebra, from the neck to the base of the spine until the arms are straight. If your hips start to come off the floor, modify the posture to rest on the elbows. Begin Breath of Fire. Continue for 1-3 minutes. Then inhale, arching the spine to the maximum. Exhale and hold the breath out briefly, apply root lock. Inhale. Exhaling slowly, lower the arms and relax the spine, vertebra by vertebra, from the base of the spine to the top. Relax, lying on the belly with the chin in the floor and the arms by the sides. This exercise balances the sexual energy and draws the prana to balance apana so that the kundalini energy can circulate to the higher centers in the following exercises.

8) Shoulder Shrugs. Sit in Easy Pose. Place the hands on the knees. Inhale and shrug the shoulders up toward the ears. Exhale and drop the shoulders down. Continue rhythmically with powerful breathing for 1-2 minutes. Inhale. Exhale and relax. This exercise balances the upper chakras and opens up the higher brain centers.

9) Neck Rolls. Sit in Easy Pose. Begin rolling the neck clockwise in a circular motion, bringing the right ear toward the right shoulder, the back of the head toward the back of the neck, the left ear toward the left shoulder and the chin toward the chest. The shoulders remain relaxed and motionless. The neck should be allowed to gently stretch as the head circles around. Continue for 1-2 minutes, then reverse the direction and continue for 1-2 minutes more. Bring the head to a central position and relax.

10) Sat Kriya. Sit on the heels with the arms overhead and the palms together. Interlace the fingers except for the index fingers, which point straight up. Men cross the right thumb over the left thumb: women cross the left thumb over the right. Begin to chant Sat Naam emphatically in a constant rhythm about 8 times per 10 seconds. Chant the sound Sat from the navel point and solar plexus, and pull the navel all the way in and up. On Naam relax the navel. Continue for 3 minutes, then inhale and pull the root lock. Mentally allow the energy to flow through the top of the skull. Exhale and hold the breath out and pull all of the locks. Inhale deeply and pull root lock. Exhale and hold the breath out and pull all the locks. Inhale and relax. Sat Kriya circulates the Kundalini energy through the cycle of the chakras, aids in digestion and strengthens the nervous system.

11) Relax on the back with the arms at the sides, palms facing up. Deep relaxation allows you to enjoy and consciously integrate the mind/body changes which have been brought about during the practice of this kriya. It allows you to sense the extension of the self through the magnetic field and the aura and allows the physical body to deeply relax.

Kirtan Kriya

Sit straight in Easy Pose.

EYE POSITION: Eyes closed with eyes gently rolled up to meditate at the Brow Point.

MANTRA: Produce the five primal sounds: *S, T, N. M. A*, in the original word form:
> SAA: Infinity, cosmos, beginning
> TAA: Life, existence
> NAA: Death, change, transformation
> MAA: Rebirth

Each repetition of the entire mantra takes 3 to 4 seconds. This is the cycle of Creation. From the Infinite comes life and individual existence. From life comes death or change. From death comes the rebirth of consciousness to the joy of the Infinite through which compassion leads back to life.

MUDRA: The elbows are straight while chanting, and the mudra changes as each fingertip touches in turn the tip of the thumb with firm pressure. On SAA, touch the index(Jupiter) finger On TAA, touch the middle (Saturn) finger On NAM, touch the ring (Sun) finger On MAA, touch the pinky (Mercury) finger

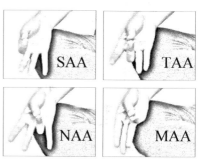

Chant in three languages of consciousness: Human: normal or loud voice (the world) Lovers: strong whisper (longing to belong) Divine: mentally: silent (Infinity)

TIME: Begin the kriya in a normal voice for 5 minutes. Then whisper for 5 minutes. Then go deep into the sound, vibrating silently for 10 minutes. Then come back to a whisper for 5 minutes, then aloud for 5 minutes. The duration of the meditation may vary, as long as the proportion of loud, whisper, silent, whisper, loud is maintained.

TO END: This sequence will take 30 minutes. Follow with one one minute of silent prayer. Then inhale, exhale. Stretch the spine, with hands up as far as possible: spread the fingers wide, taking several deep breaths. Relax.

COMMENTS Each time the mudra is closed by joining the thumb with a finger. the ego "seals" the effect of that mudra in the consciousness.

The effects are as follows:
    1st finger: Gyan Mudra: Knowledge
    2nd finger: Shuni Mudra: Wisdom, intelligence, patience
    3rd finger: Surya Mudra: Vitality, energy of life
    4th finger: Buddhi Mudra: Ability to communicate

This meditation brings a total mental balance to the individual psyche. Vibrating on each fingertip alternates the electrical polarities. The index and ring fingers are electrically negative, relative to the other fingers. This causes a balance in the electromagnetic projection of the aura.

CHECKPOINTS FOR KIRTAN KRIYA:

► If during the silent part of the meditation, the mind wanders uncontrollably, go back to a whisper, to a loud voice, to a whisper, and back into silence. Do this as often as you need to.

► If this meditation gives you a headache, meditate using the "L" form. Feel the sound coming in through the 7th chakra at the top of your head, and then making an "L" turn and beaming out through the Third Eye Point as it is projected to Infinity. This energy flow follows the energy pathway called the Golden Cord—the connection between the pineal and pituitary glands. You may also want to try covering the head with a natural fiber cloth.

Healing Meditation

Sit in an Easy Pose.

MUDRA: Have the elbows tucked comfortably against the ribs. Extend the forearms out at a 45-degree angle out from the center of the body. The palms are flat,. facing up, the wrists pulled back, fingers together, and thumbs spread. Consciously keep the palms flat during the meditation.

MANTRA: The mantra consists of eight basic sounds:

RAA MAA DAA **SAA**, SAA SAY SO **HUNG**

Punch the 4th (SAA) and 8th (HUNG) sounds by pulling in the Navel Point. Note that HUNG is not long and drawn out. Clip it off forcefully as you pull in the navel. Chant one complete cycle of the entire mantra, and then inhale deeply and repeat. To chant this mantra properly, remember to move the mouth fully with each sound. Feel the resonance in the mouth and the sinus areas. Let your mind concentrate on the qualities that are evoked by the combination of sounds.

TIME: Chant powerfully for 11-31 minutes.

TO END: Inhale deeply and hold the breath as you offer a healing prayer, visualizing the person you wish to heal (including yourself) as being totally healthy, radiant, and strong. Imagine the person completely engulfed in healing white light, completely healed. Then exhale and inhale deeply again, hold the breath and offer your prayer. Then, lift your arms up high and vigorously shake out your hands and fingers.

COMMENTS Certain mantras are to be cherished like the most rare and beautiful gem. This mantra is just such a find. It is unique, and it captures the radiant healing energy of the Cosmos as a gem captures the light of the sun. And like a gem it can be put into many settings for different purposes and occasions.

Each of these eight sounds has a unique energy and vibration:

- RAA means the energy of the sun: strong. bright, and hot. It energizes and purifies.
- MAA is the energy of the moon. It is a quality of receptivity, coolness, and nurturing.

- DAA is the energy of Earth. It is secure, personal, and grounding.
- SAA is Infinity.

Then the mantra repeats the sound: this repetition is a turning point. The first part of the mantra is ascending and expands into the Infinite. The second brings the energy back down. It interweaves the ether with the earth!

- SAA is Infinity.
- SAY which is the totality of personal experience.
- SO is the personal sense of identity.
- HUNG is the Infinite brought to the personal level.

As you chant this mantra you complete a cycle of energy and go through a circuit of the chakras. You grow toward the Infinite and then you bring that infinite vibration back from the impersonal to the personal level.

Prosperity meditation

Sit in Easy Pose.

EYE POSITION: Focus at the tip of the nose, through eyes 9/10th closed.

MUDRA: Hit first one side of the hands together and then the other side. The Mercury (pinky) fingers and the Moon Mounds (fleshy mounds below the pinkies) hit when the palms are facing up. Then the thumbs fold under the hands and the Jupiter (index) fingers and the thumb knuckles hit under the hands when the palms are facing down.

MANTRA: The Tantric Har tape is perfect for this meditation. Chant the mantra HAR continuously from the navel about once a second. Make sure the tip of the tongue flicks the upper palate to make the "R" sound. It will actually sound more like a "D"

TIME: Continue for 3-31 minutes.

COMMENTS: This is what Yogi Bhajan said about this meditation: "This meditation stimulates the mind, the moon center and Jupiter. When Jupiter and the moon come together, there is no way in the world you will not create wealth."

Yogi Tea

Good for the blood, liver, nervous system, and bones. Good for colds, flu, and physical weakness.

> 10 ounces (315 ml) water
> 2 slices fresh ginger root (optional. but excellent!)
> 3 cloves
> 4 green cardamon pods. cracked
> 4 black peppercorns
> 1/2 stick cinnamon
> 1/4 teaspoon black tea (a teabag)
> 1/2 cup (125 ml) milk or equivalent
> Honey, to taste (optional)

Bring the water to a boil and add the spices. Cover and continue boiling for 10-15 minutes. Remove from heat, add black tea, and let steep for 1-2 minutes. Add honey and milk, bring back to a boil and then remove from heat. Strain and serve. This recipe is for one cup, but you can make it by the gallon using the same proportions.

Mung Beans & Rice with Vegetables

This is a perfectly balanced protein dish, easy to digest, and very satisfying. Good any time of the year, but especially good in the winter.

> 4-1/2 cups (1.25 L) water
> 1/2 cup (250 ml) mung beans
> 1/2 cup (250 mi) basmati rice
> 1/4 cup (125 ml) ginger root, finely minced
> 1 onion, chopped
> 3 cloves garlic, minced
> 3 cups chopped vegetables
> 2 Tablespoons (40 ml) ghee or vegetable oil
> 3/4 teaspoon turmeric
> 1/4 teaspoon crushed red chilies
> 1/4 teaspoon ground black pepper
> 1/2 teaspoon ground coriander
> 1/2 teaspoon ground garam masala
> 1/2 teaspoon ground cumin
> 1/4 teaspoon. cardamom seeds (2 pods)
> 1 bay leaf

Rinse mung beans and rice. Add mung beans to boiling water and cook until beans begin to split. Add rice and cook another 15 minutes, stirring occasionally. Now add the vegetables. (Alternatively, one could add the vegetables along with the rice.) As the mixture cooks, it will start to thicken.

Heat the ghee or vegetable oil in a frying pan. Add onions, ginger, and garlic and sauté until clear. Add spices and cook 5 more minutes, stirring constantly. Add a little water if necessary. Add this to the rice and beans. The final consistency should be like a thick soup. Total cooking time is about 1-1/2 hours. Add salt or soy sauce to taste. Serve plain or with yogurt. Makes 4 servings.

Potent Potatoes

This recipe has its roots in the tradition of yogic cooking. The spices help to purify the blood, stimulate digestion, and increase energy. You may decrease the amounts of pepper and cayenne to suit your taste.

4 large baking potatoes
1/4-1/2 cup (65-125 ml) ghee or vegetable oil
2-3 onions, chopped
1/4-1/2 cup (65-125 ml) ginger root, minced
1-2 Tablespoons (20-40 ml) garlic, minced
1/4 tsp. caraway seeds
1 tsp. black pepper
3/4-1 tsp. turmeric
1 tsp. cayenne or crushed red chilies
8 whole cloves
1/2 tsp ground cardamom
1/4 tsp ground cinnamon
Soy sauce or salt to taste
1/2 pint (500 ml) cottage cheese
1/2 pound (225 gr) cheese, grated
1 red or green bell pepper, diced
1/2 cup (125 ml) chopped pineapple, drained

Scrub potatoes, rub with small amount of oil and bake at 400° (200° C) until well done. Heat ghee or oil in a large skillet. Sauté onions and ginger until they begin to brown, then add garlic and spices and cook for 4-5 minutes longer. Add a little water if necessary. Add soy sauce. Stir and remove from heat.

Cut baked potatoes in half, lengthwise. Scoop out the insides and combine with onion mixture. Add cottage cheese. Mix well and refill potato shells, covering each with grated cheese. Broil until cheese is melted and bubbly. For a nice touch, garnish with bell pepper and pineapple. Serve with yogurt. Makes 4 potent potatoes.

Beet & Carrot Casserole

This dish is cleansing to the liver and the digestive tract.

   1 bunch beets
   1 pound carrots
   2 bunches scallions, chopped
   3 cloves garlic, minced
   ghee or vegetable oil
   soy sauce
   ground black pepper
   grated cheese

Scrub beets and carrots. Cut off end of root and stems. Steam beets whole. Peel carrots and steam separately. Steam both until tender but firm. Remove outer peels from beets. They should squirt out of their skins. Grate using a coarse grater. Keep beets and carrots separate to preserve their distinct colors.

Sauté scallions and garlic in oil or ghee until tender. Toss with beets, carrots and black pepper. Place in casserole dish. Sprinkle with soy sauce. Cover with grated cheese and broil until cheese is melted and golden. Serves 4-6.

3HO – Healthy Happy Holy Organization

http://www.3ho.org/

This is the first website to start your exploration. You will find a wealth of information about Kundalini Yoga all over the world: database of all teachers worldwide , events, meditations and kriyas, yogic lifestyle, etc.

KRI – Kundalini Research Institute

http://kundaliniresearchinstitute.org/

KRI oversees Kundalini yoga teacher training. On this site you will find: kriyas and meditations, mantra pronunciation, and info on teacher training.

White Tantric Yoga

http://www.whitetantricyoga.com/

You will find more information about White Tantric yoga on this website as well as a list of upcoming courses.

Yogi Bhajan

http://www.yogibhajan.org/

This site has information about Yogi Bhajan: pictures, stories, and the library of his lectures and classes that he taught from 1969 to 2004.

Library of Teachings

http://www.libraryofteachings.com/

Yogi Bhajan taught thousands of classes and all were recorded. Many of these have been transcribed and you can read, watch, or listen to the master on this website. Pick a new lecture to watch once or twice a week.

Sikhnet

http://www.sikhnet.com/

This site has more information about the Sikh religion.

Kundalini Treasures

http://www.kundalinitreasures.com/

This book is part of a series of education tools that have been created by Santokh Singh Khalsa, D.C. In addition to this book, he also has created two CDs. These can be ordered on this website:

> **Mantras of the Master** is a recording of 64 different mantras taught by Yogi Bhajan. The CD comes with a booklet with an explanation of each mantra.

> **A Simple Yoga Practice**. This CD and booklet will help you get started with a daily practice. The CD is modular so you can start with a short practice and as you increase your practice, you add more of the CD tracks.

Other online sites to order books, music, and DVDs:

Yogatech: http://yogatech.com/

Spirit Voyage: http://www.spiritvoyage.com/

Ancient Healing Ways: http://www.a-healing.com/